Rise Up Military Moms

A JOURNAL FOR LIVING
LIFE WITH STRENGTH AND PURPOSE

Army Mom Strong and Elaine Brye

Copyright © 2018 Army Mom Strong and Elaine Brye

All rights reserved. No part of this book may be used or reproduced by any means, graphic, electronic, or mechanical, including photocopying, recording, taping, or by any information storage retrieval system without the written permission of the authors except in the case of brief quotations embodied in critical articles and reviews.

Printed in the United States of America

Rise Up Military Moms

HeartofaMilitaryMom.com

ISBN-13: 978-1985694453

ISBN-10: 198569445X

Dedication

For all the military moms out there
standing strong in their love for their children,
and to our own children who inspire us every day.

Contents

	Acknowledgments	vii
	Introduction	1
1	Release	3
2	Research	15
3	Reclaim	27
4	Renew	37
5	Recreate	47
6	Represent	57
	We Stand Watch	67
	Connections	68
	About the Authors	69

Acknowledgments

A special thank you goes out to all the military moms who continue to inspire us on the journey of a lifetime!

We are thankful to friends Richard, Keiko and Diane for reading every word of this journal and going through the guidance.

We are so grateful for the online military mom communities that help us all connect and know that *we are all in this together.*

*We share the greatest pride,
the greatest fear and the greatest faith.
And we do this together.*

~ Army Mom Strong

Introduction

I don't think I can explain what it's like to send your child off to transition from civilian to military member or send them off to a combat deployment.

As a mom, it's a high stress, emotional roller coaster full of unknowns and fear. I felt that way when my son was deployed and I knew he was getting fired upon in every mission.

My thoughts became unbearable at times as my fears continued to steal away more of me.

I made it my mission to conquer my fears, build up my strength, and find joy in this military mom journey.

When Elaine and I first met, we discovered that we shared a similar path to Rise Up in our own lives amid the emotional ups and downs.

This book is the result of the steps we both took to gain strength and become more FEAR-less.

Rise Up is aimed at helping you find strength and resilience over the next 6 months of weekly guided journaling. We focused on these six areas that helped us the most:

Release: Letting go

Research: Knowledge is power

Reclaim: Finding joy in your journey

Renew: Energize your spirit

Recreate: Focus on your strength and resilience

Represent: Educate and support your community

Each week features ways in which you can take action to awaken your strength, energize your spirit, and face your fears.

You'll also find positive insights to help inspire and uplift you through your military mom journey. Additional blank note pages are provided in each section for writing any reflections, thoughts, and introspections.

As you go through this journal, know that you are amazing! You raised an incredible person that is a member of the smartest and best trained military in the world.

Remember that you are the brave one who raised a warrior!

Release

LETTING GO CAN BE HARD

You've probably heard it a hundred times. You just need to let go. We know that in our hearts. I can remember when my four year old said to me, "Momma I'm going to be Top Gun someday." He was already planning his future beyond our back yard. That's a good thing isn't it? We want our children to dream and work toward their best selves.

But sometimes the reality of that can be painful, especially if you are a military mom. It is hard to let go of your child to a life as a warrior and all that entails. We spend our lives protecting them from danger and then one day they come home and say, "I enlisted" or "I am joining ROTC" and your heart swells and drops at the same time. I was and am so proud of my four military service members, but contemplating them in danger is a lot to take in.

How do you release your child to all that means?

It starts with basic training and continues until they are the tip of the spear, on the front lines of our nation's defense and most likely deployed in dangerous places or doing dangerous things.

How do we cope?

It all goes back to releasing and letting go of our children. It hurts. It's messy. But there are ways to do it with grace. In this section of Rise Up we share some strategies and guide you to find your best way to meet this first challenge.

It does not matter if you are a new military mom or if this is your fifth deployment. We can practice being brave every day and cultivate a fresh way of approaching the role loving our military children brings.

I do miss my babies. I miss the feel of their soft cheeks against mine, the smell of a freshly bathed bundle of joy, the knowledge that their world begins and ends with me. But that time is past. And if I spend too much energy reflecting on it I can be brought to a dark place of melancholy.

They are not my babies anymore. They are grown men and women with dreams and motivations to excel.

They have worked hard to become who they are and the difficult trainings they endure make them stronger and more capable. The sooner I stop thinking of them as my babies the more I see them as who they truly are: warriors who excel.

When the worries of the night engulf me: is the drill sergeant too hard, is the deployment too dangerous? I focus instead on the stubborn persistent child who would not let go of his or her dreams. It is all a matter of perspective.

When you change the way you think about them it becomes much easier to start celebrating who they are becoming instead of mourning the loss of their childhood.

There are practical ways to help you change your attitude. I moved the baby pictures to the basement and keep pictures of them getting their wings or graduating. When they left I did not keep their bedrooms as a shrine to their childhood. I needed that sewing room anyway!

Acknowledging they have moved on has been harder on me than them by the way. In each case they have had little interest in keeping the mounds of memorabilia I carefully packed away. It's a great lesson for me to celebrate where and who they are now.

I acknowledge my feelings. Fear and anxiety are certainly present, but I work to replace them with positive thoughts. I create my own slogans and positive affirmations that help beat back the negative emotions.

Some of the pep talks I give myself when the emotional surge hits me:

"No news is good news"

"I'm a warrior too"

"My child is among the best the world"

There are certainly moments of sentimentality and I allow myself to indulge in them occasionally. But I know this for sure: my children need me to support them and what they are doing now. When I wish they are all home and underfoot I am not helpful to them.

I need to remember that when releasing seems too hard. The best mother I can be is one who lifts them up even if it means they are moving further and further away from me.

Take Action

- What are some of the obstacles you have to releasing your children?
- What are some practical steps you can practice this month to help you let go?
- Where can you find strength in the process?
- How can you transition with grace?

_____
_____
_____
_____
_____
_____
_____

When sadness overcomes me, I let those moments be moments and carry on.

~ *Army Mom Strong*

I can be brave and courageous.

I can take care of myself by relaxing.

I will create positive memories in my life.

I can be brave and strong.

1 Release
Letting go can be hard

♡ ♡ ♡ ♡ ♡

I am Feeling ...

Identify the Source of My Feelings

Amazing Things that Happened this Week

Weekly Goal
o o o o o o o

Starve fear and feed hope. ~ Elaine Brye

2 Release *find your positive energy fuel*

♡ ♡ ♡ ♡ ♡

I Feel Proud About ...

Gratitude List

Positive Things that Happened this Week

Weekly Goal
o o o o o o o

3 Release *Create affirmations*

♡ ♡ ♡ ♡ ♡

Ways I Can Be Brave

Positive Inspirations

Weekly Goal
○ ○ ○ ○ ○ ○ ○

Affirmations that Helped this Week

4 Release — *Transition with grace*

Things I Look Forward To

Ways to Change Negative Thoughts to Positive

Weekly Goal

Ways I Moved Forward this Week

We get stronger because it does not get easier. ~ *Elaine Brye*

We are all in this together

You can do this!

Military Mom: Powered by Pride

Research

KNOWLEDGE IS POWER

I really thought I knew it all. I grew up in the military, trained in the military, and married someone in the military. How could this military mom stuff be so hard?

But the moment my first child raised his hand and took his oath to protect and defend the Constitution I was undone. I was completely disoriented and blindsided by the emotional surge that buffeted me.

Looking back now I see how it was so similar to the dunk tank training my aviators were subjected to. Strapped into a simulated cockpit their "aircraft" descended into a pool as it twisted and turned. Then they had to find their way to the surface.

If you ever watched the movie "An Officer and a Gentleman," there is a very realistic depiction of this training.

The grasping for the seat belts and trying to determine which way is up while trying to hold my breath describes my early days as a military mom.

Finding my way to the surface got much harder after 9/11. I became a military mom during peacetime and now all semblance of calm was gone. What do you do when you feel like your world is spinning around and that your child (or children) are caught up in the maelstrom? I went back to my roots. I remember my mom quoting that age-old adage to me, "Knowledge is power."

As a child, we researched every new military post to which we moved. There were twenty-two. Mom forced us to immerse ourselves in the new cultures and learn. The result was that I learned to navigate the unfamiliar until it became comfortable.

I brought that scholarly approach to this new world of being a military mom, and it made all the difference.

What do I mean by knowledge is power? The more you know and understand the less fearful it is.

The first step when your child leaves for military service or a deployment is to get your bearings. Just like in the dunk tank, you need to find which way is up. Learn about your child's new world. Start with the acronyms. It's those initials that make up a whole new language. Go to the military base page where they are stationed and read what is going on there. You will find tons of information to provide perspective.

Find some guides like other moms or veterans who can really explain the nuts and bolts to you. Look for positive sources of information, not people who are jaded and negative about their experiences. Remember childbirth? You don't listen to the horror stories. Instead find people who can give you balanced information.

Study their new destination. If stateside, look for things to do in the area, or cultural events. Be prepared when they complain there is nothing to do. If they are deploying overseas research that country.

Understanding the culture and history can give you a great perspective on their service there. Get a map and get to know their surroundings. There is something very comforting about being able to picture where they are especially if they are not good at sending photos like my children were!

Read books on the military experience. Search out factual accounts, not fictitious novels. Read the online news from Military Times or Stars and Stripes. It will fill in the blanks you might have since most of our mainstream newspapers and magazines do not have a military perspective.

When I was pregnant the first thing I did was research. I wanted to understand what was happening and what a legitimate worry was. My guidebook during that time was "What to Expect When You are Expecting."

Then, as my children arrived I consumed books about child development. The information gave me peace of mind. I so wished I had something like that as I started this military mom journey.

It is one reason I wrote "Be Safe, Love Mom: A Military Mom's Guide to Courage, Comfort and Surviving Life on the Homefront."

But there is no one book that can take you everywhere your children will go. It's up to you to gather the information to make your heart stop racing and find your way. It will make all the difference in this military mom journey.

It made a huge difference for me and helped me push through the fears that kept me awake at night.

Take Action

- What tools can you use to get your bearings?
- How can you find a reliable guide or mentor in your community?
- What are some great resources you can use to learn more about the military and your children's new world?

Embrace new challenges and adventures in life to help carry the burden of worry.

~ Elaine Brye

I will continue to learn and grow.

I surround myself with positive people.

I stay persistent in my quest to learn.

I gain strength from difficulties.

1 Research *get your bearings*

My Greatest Fear About Learning

Ways I Can Push Through My Fears ★

Weekly Goal

Things I Learned About Military Life this Week

With the help & support of friends, lean into it and embrace this journey. ~ Army Mom Strong

2 Research *finding guidance*

Online Resources

Good Advice I got from Others ★

Weekly Goal

Helpful People I Connected With this Week

3 Research
Researching duty station

What Holds me Back From Learning

My Child's Job & Mission is...

Weekly Goal
o o o o o o o

Ways that Research Helped Me to Understand More this Week

4 Research *Knowledge is power!*

Books to Read

Online Military News Sources

How New Knowledge Helped me this Week

Weekly Goal

The more you know and understand the less fearful it is. ~ Elaine Brye

Learning is a treasure

Keep smiling

Learning is an adventure

Reclaim

FINDING JOY IN YOUR JOURNEY

When was the last time you experienced real joy that had nothing to do with your child or grandchildren? Have you lost sight of who you are beyond Mom? As we grapple with our children moving out in the world and the anxieties that accompany that change, we might realize that we left someone behind.

Who did we leave behind? The non-mom part of us.

I can remember my own mom pushing me to get my teacher certification in my forties. I had a houseful of kids and was busy every second of the day.

Why did I need one more thing to do?

Later as the children left one by one, I realized her wisdom. She knew I needed to pour my passion into something else. In this case it was teaching to fill the emptiness they left behind.

Who knew it would carry me to the ends of the earth in Afghanistan and open up so many new possibilities? It was a blessing to have a part of me that extended beyond my intensive parenting years. It also gave me valuable insights into my children's deployment world that helped me understand why sometimes they need to be distant from the ones they love.

I'm not suggesting you need to go back to school or go to a war zone. But who knows what you might do if you give yourself time to think about it.

When your life is consumed with raising children there's not much room to consider the possibilities.

Now as the house begins to empty out there is nothing to stop you from dreaming. Big dreams or small ones, it really doesn't matter. The key is to start thinking about who you are and what you want to be going forward. We all can create a second act.

Your children are forging their path. They are doing hard things, pushing past barriers, and stretching themselves. Those hard training and trials like the Marine Crucible can keep us up at night. But they will be so proud of their accomplishments. We can also be proud of the steps we take to move forward.

> One of the biggest protective factors in dealing with the changes and stress of living life as a military mom is taking the time to find yourself.

What makes you happy besides your family? What are you passionate about? What goals would you like to set for yourself? The sky is the limit.

It's not selfish. It is planning for the life you would like to have after your children are gone.

We never think to do that.

Life is so hectic is seems like it will always be this way and then they are gone. The worry can beat like a loud drum in an empty room.

I'm grateful my mom was wise enough to point the way for me. The new challenges and adventures have certainly helped my carry the burden as I miss my children and worry about their safety.

Take Action

- What would you like to reclaim?
- What brings you joy on a daily basis?
- What are some things you would like to start working toward?
- How can you turn worry into something productive?

People are just as happy as they make up their minds to be.

~ Abraham Lincoln

I am more aware of what I want for me.

I do things that make me happy.

I explore new things.

I create joy every day in my life.

1 Reclaim *finding your joy*

★ ★ ★ ★ ★
What Joy Means to Me

Things that Nourish my Spirit

_____
_____
_____
_____
_____
_____
_____
_____

Weekly Goal
o o o o o o o

Ways I Found Joy this Week

True happiness is to enjoy the present without anxious dependence upon the future.
~ Lucius Annaeus Seneca

2 Reclaim — *Deciding what you want*

★ ★ ★ ★ ★

MY PURPOSE IN LIFE IS ...

MY UNIQUE QUALITIES

_____
_____
_____
_____
_____
_____
_____
_____

WEEKLY GOAL

o o o o o o o o

NEW THINGS I THOUGHT ABOUT THIS WEEK

3 Reclaim — *Moving forward*

★ ★ ★ ★ ★
New things I Want to Do

Steps I can Take to Move Forward

_____
_____
_____
_____
_____
_____
_____
_____

Weekly Goal
o o o o o o o o

Ways I Made a Difference this Week

4 Reclaim — *Celebrating you!*

★ ★ ★ ★ ★
I am Proud of Myself For

Things I did Towards my BIG Dream

_____
_____
_____
_____
_____
_____
_____
_____

Weekly Goal
○ ○ ○ ○ ○ ○ ○ ○

Things I did to Take Care of Me this Week

Let's celebrate something today!

Reclaim, recreate, and rejuvenate

Have the courage to keep moving forward

Renew

ENERGIZE YOUR SPIRIT

As my children left the nest, the void they left was immense. After spending more than twenty years preparing them to leave, I had done virtually nothing to prepare myself. Perhaps you are a mom like I was, using most of your energy to take care of and nurture family.

I put myself on the back burner and used all my energy just to keep up with all the demands my life entailed. Now facing a big paradigm change, I finally had time for myself.

It was time for renewal.

As I contemplated things I wanted to change, I had to figure out what I had the power to change. Nothing I did would bring my children home or return things to the way they used to be.

And did I really want that?

I take much joy in watching them live the lives they have worked hard for. As I focused on me for a change, I had the desire to create a new life in four different categories: physical, emotional, spiritual and connections.

The first was physical. I really want to be around to see my grandchildren grow up and to keep up with my busy family. Getting stronger physically is a new priority for me. I have always struggled with making this a priority.

But now I have more time than I did in the past. I also discovered that physical activity helps lift the weight of worry. It's a fact that exercise helps reduce stress, and I can attest to that.

There is nothing like lacing up my walking shoes and heading out the door to walk away from the cares of the day. I can feel those cares falling off my shoulders as I listen to the birds, all the while experiencing the sights and sounds of the mountain where I live.

During some deployments I have imagined myself walking to the country where my child is stationed. Other times I just logged steps against worry. I will never be a super model but getting stronger physically makes me stronger mentally, and I need all the strength I can get.

Focusing on emotional renewal, I make an effort to remove any thing that is toxic in my world.

Energy zappers in the form of selfish relationships or negativity have no room in my heart. It is too full of pride and anxiety. I focus on the positive and look for joy as much as I can.

Spiritual renewal helps me draw closer to my God. Prayer is an essential part of my day. I also carve out time for solitude. No matter what your faith is, time alone and taking time to be mindful can calm a restless spirit. At one time in my life five minutes of solitude was unheard of, but now I can take the time to unplug and rest.

Connection has become even more important as my house has emptied out. But it is not the quantity of connections but the quality is what matters.

Finding friends who truly understand the demands on my heart is essential. It may take an effort to find them but when you do it is well worth it. What better way to calm a restless spirit than to go for a walk with a true friend!

All of this has contributed to helping me live a more balanced life in the face of fears that only a military mom can understand.

Take Action

- What are some ways you can seek to renew your life?
- What goals can you set to improve your physical well-being?
- What are strategies you can implement to guard your heart?
- What are practices you can use to renew your spirit?
- How can you develop better connections?

_____
_____
_____
_____
_____
_____
_____
_____

Anxiety tears you down, faith builds you up.

~ The Heart of a Military Mom

I have the ability to change anything in my life.

I surround myself with positive, authentic people.

I maintain balance in mind, body, and spirit.

I replenish my strength by taking care of me.

1 Renew — *Restoring physical well-being*

Is my Physical Well-being a Source of Joy or Burden

Ways I Can Be More Active Daily

_____
_____
_____
_____
_____
_____
_____
_____

Things I did to Take Responsibility for my Physical Well-being this Week

Weekly Goal

When you arise in the morning, think of what a precious privilege it is to be alive – to breathe, to think, to enjoy, to love. ~ Marcus Aurelius

2 Renew *cultivating emotional well-being*

Stuff that Weighs me Down

Ways I Can Lighten the Load

Things I did to practice Mindfulness this Week

Weekly Goal

3 Renew *creating a strong spiritual foundation*

Ways I Can Feel Peaceful & Calm

Things I Marvel at in Everyday Life

How I Strengthened my Spiritual Connection this Week

Weekly Goal

4 Renew — *Making meaningful connections*

Ways I can Develop True Friendships

What do Deep Connections Mean to Me

How I Was Helpful or Unforgettable to Others this Week

Weekly Goal

When you give yourself, you receive more than you give. ~ Antoine de Saint-Exupery

Relax, refresh, and renew

Face the challenges ahead with joy

Recreate

FOCUS ON YOUR STRENGTH AND RESILIENCE

As I struggled to cope with all the changes that came with being drafted into my new role as a military mom I realized I had a choice. I could succumb to the worries and the fear and spend my days complaining and wishing things were like the old days.

Or I could *Rise Up* to create a new attitude and approach to living my life. We are never too old to recreate ourselves and start again.

It is just not easy being a military mom. I knew I needed a new approach to harden my armor as life got tougher.

My first step was to stop treating my children as my babies. They are trained as accomplished adult warriors. I needed to treat them as fellow adults. It can be hard to drop that mindset.

Those baby days were some of my most precious memories. But they are not babies anymore. I found the more I honored them for who they are now the easier it was for me to accept what they do.

Picturing my toddler alone in a foreign country in harm's way is excruciating. Focusing on how brave and accomplished they are gives me great comfort. On difficult days I stay away from the baby photos and childhood art projects. Instead, I look at photos of them getting their wings or graduating. They can do these hard things they are called to do and so can I.

Fear. It is something we live with when we love someone who may be in harm's way. I practice being FEARLESS, that is FEAR-Less with a hyphen. I work at reducing my fear in many ways.

I go outside more to walk and be active. Something about getting away and just moving helps to calm my mind. I get creative. The act of knitting or quilting transports me to another place where I can drop my cares for a while. When I feel overcome I reach out to a friend who understands.

> Being FEAR-Less does not just happen. We need to practice being brave. I try to put more energy into positives rather than negatives.

I avoid energy drainers because it takes work to keep those worries at bay. You need to commit to fighting the fears and to work at being fearless. Just like a weightlifter keeps lifting weights to build their muscles, we need to build our brave muscles.

It's easy to instill a great amount of fear in my heart and mind, especially when my service member is deployed to a war zone. It's harder to tackle my fears head-on.

It was important to recognize the things I can and cannot control in my life. I cannot control my child's career or where it takes him. I can control my own actions and responses.

I found a way to replace many of my fears with the same excitement and passion that my son shared with me about his various missions. As I understood more about his passion for serving, I could feel confidence and bravery growing in my heart.

Never forget that you raised a warrior. You were the one they depended on to keep their fears at bay. You scared away the monsters under the bed and reassured them as they took their scary first steps.

Now that they are out in the world they still need to know that you are someone they can depend on. It's what we mommas do.

Take Action

- How can you work to create a new attitude?
- What are some practical things you can do to practice being brave?
- How can you encourage yourself when the going gets tough?
- What are ways you can prioritize yourself?

The only way to deal with fear is to face it and push through it.

~ Elaine Brye

I radiate positive energy.

I focus on being brave and bold.

I let go of my fear of the unknown.

I change my fears into excitement and passion.

1 Recreate — *Honoring my adult child*

Ways I can Recognize my Child as a Warrior

How to observe Respectful boundaries

_____
_____
_____
_____
_____
_____
_____
_____

Weekly Goal
○ ○ ○ ○ ○ ○ ○ ○

Positive Ways I Connected with my child this Week

We are never too old to recreate ourselves and start again. ~ Elaine Brye

2 Recreate *Building up strength*

Recognize the Fears in my Life

How Can I Overcome my Fears?

Weekly Goal
○ ○ ○ ○ ○ ○ ○

Ways I Amplified my Inner Strength this Week

3 Recreate *Practicing being brave*

Things I Can Control in Life

Ways I Can Adapt to New Changes

Weekly Goal
o o o o o o o o

Proud Moments of Being Brave this Week

4 Recreate — *Defining who I am*

Ways I can Invest in Me

How I can Approach Life in a New way

Weekly Goal
○ ○ ○ ○ ○ ○ ○

Valuable Lessons Learned About Me this Week

We cannot solve our problems with the same thinking we used when we created them. ~ *Albert Einstein*

Bloom with grace

Be strong, be fear-less, be beautiful

Represent

EDUCATE AND SUPPORT

The military civilian divide is a buzzword you hear a lot if you spend much time researching military and veteran's issues. The fact that so many Americans are out of touch with the challenges and sacrifices of military members and those who love them is not a mystery to us.

We get it every day. "WEAR RED to Remember Everyone Deployed" is a valiant effort to remind our friends and neighbors that yes, we still are fighting wars and our children are being deployed every day.

The reality is that most people just don't understand.

A big contributor to the lack of understanding is so many folks just don't have a personal connection anymore. In statistics, we see the all-volunteer armed forces have limited the population who serves.

The number of people who have a current family member in the military is less than twenty percent compared to a generation ago when most families had family members serving in the military.

While it can be very annoying to deal with the lack of connection and support, we can do something about it. Instead of wasting our energy complaining or being offended we can make a difference.

We can represent. We can tell our children's stories and work to bridge the gap between civilians and the military. The end result is a better country for all of us.

There are ways to educate others about the reality of life on the homefront. We cannot expect folks to just know. We need to teach them. Sometimes that is in the form of frank conversations but there are other ways to share.

Visiting schools and teaching children about your sons or daughters service can be a great way to instruct the next generation. Visiting veteran organizations and hospitals can be a wonderful way to learn the stories of neighborhood heroes which you can pass on.

As you educate yourself you can also get involved and advocate for our children and their families. A call to your Congressman and Senator is something you can do that can make a difference. There are multiple organizations you can join that work on veteran and military issues. We need to make our voices loud and proud. I liken it to being a grizzly bear momma. I will do anything to protect my cubs. We can be a force for good just like our children are.

There is also a lot of pent up momma energy that can be put to good use as we adjust to the empty nest. Veterans' hospitals can always use more volunteers. The American Red Cross, Disabled American Veterans, Veterans of Foreign Wars, and veteran-based homeless initiatives are just a few organizations that come to mind that can use your energy and talents.

> One of the best things you can do as you travel this military mom journey is to pay it forward.

There are new moms being drafted into the military mom role every day. They need your wisdom and expertise. They need to know they are not crazy and that they are not alone. Reaching out and bringing them alongside is one of the greatest gifts you can give them. Where would we be without our battle buddies?

"Be All You Can Be" was the Army's slogan for 21 years. It inspired a nation of young people to become their best by entering into military service.

As a military mom, I will continue to "be all I can be." Let's be a shining example to others through kindness and grace, and be our best!

Ultimately it will make all the difference to the ones you love the most.

Take Action

- How can you step up and use your energy and wisdom to represent?
- Can you teach others in a loving way about the military community and help others to understand it better?
- How can you make a difference wherever you are?
- How can you be a shining example to others through kindness and grace?

_____
_____
_____
_____
_____
_____
_____

Be a shining example to others through kindness and grace, and be our best!

~ Rise Up

I use my knowledge and wisdom for the good of all.

I strive to be the best I can be.

I am a good role model to others.

I appreciate others for being a positive part of my life.

1 Represent *Educating others*

♡ ♡ ♡ ♡ ♡

Ways I Can Help Others Understand

Things People Ask About My Child

How I Educated Others this Week

Weekly Goal

○ ○ ○ ○ ○ ○ ○ ○

The real passion of the twentieth century is servitude. ~ Albert Camus

2 Represent — *Advocate for our military*

Local & National Organizations I can Support

♡ ♡ ♡ ♡ ♡

Contact Info for my Congressman and Senator

_____
_____
_____
_____
_____
_____
_____
_____

Weekly Goal

o o o o o o o o

New Ways I Spread Awareness about the Military Community this Week

3 Represent *Volunteering to help*

♡ ♡ ♡ ♡ ♡

What I want to Do to Help

Steps I can Take to volunteer

_____
_____
_____
_____
_____
_____
_____
_____

Weekly Goal

o o o o o o o

Ways I Made a Difference This Week

4 Represent  *Supporting military moms*

♡ ♡ ♡ ♡ ♡
Ways to Connect with Military Moms

Things I can do to Support Others

Weekly Goal
o o o o o o o o

Ways I Supported a Military Mom This Week

We rise by lifting others. ~ Robert Ingersoll

Lift up others

Represent through your positive energy and wisdom

We Stand Watch

"We stand watch on our post night after night, day after day, because of the overwhelming pride we feel knowing that it is our children who carry the banner of freedom; this is what helps us endure all those sleepless nights. We fight back all our worries and fears because we love our country.

We love our country enough to give our children up. We love this nation and its principles enough to stand and say, "Take my precious child and make him or her a warrior."

We know that our sons and daughters are worthy of our respect and gratitude, and we accept they have been called to fight for freedom.

We know what it took to get them to where they are today—the bravery, the stamina, the sacrifices, the guts. We raised them. We had a front row seat.

So here's to all the unsung heroes—those mommas who have had the guts to let go, toughen up, remain Semper Gumby, embrace the suck, and carry on. I am proud to serve with you."

Printed with Permission from "Be Safe, Love Mom: A Military Mom's Stories of Courage, Comfort, and Surviving Life on the Home Front" by Elaine Brye

Resources & Connections

We hope you find these resources and ways to connect helpful.

Heart of a Military Mom helps military moms face fears through value, perspective, and inspiration.

HeartofaMilitaryMom.com

Facebook.com/heartofamilitarymom

Army Mom Strong provides support, resources, and prayer to families of Army service members.

ArmyMomStrong.com

Facebook.com/armymomstrong

Be Safe, Love Mom supports and connects those who love and support their military children. Her website is based on the philosophy of her acclaimed book, "Be Safe, Love Mom."

BeSafeLoveMom.com

Facebook.com/besafelovemom

About the Authors

The authors co-created "Rise Up" to share the journey and steps they took to build their own strength and resilience amid the emotional ups and downs of life as a military mom.

When Lisa's son prepared for a deployment, she shed many tears amid sleepless nights. Feeling alone and unprepared, she scoured the Internet to educate herself about the mission over there, in a strange mix of fear and pride. She knew there were others who felt the same way.

She founded Army Mom Strong, an online Facebook community of over 95,000 that supports moms and family of Army service members.

Over the years, she learned to find joy in this journey whether it be deployments, or overseas and stateside duty assignments, while strengthening her inner resolve.

She is fiercely dedicated to her family and enjoys traveling the globe for frequent visits with her family, wherever they may be. She is an avid runner, passionate about living a healthy lifestyle and helps others do the same through natural solutions.

Her adventures as an Army Mom over the years led her to create "The Heart of a Military Mom" with co-author Elaine Brye to help inspire others who are on this journey.

Elaine Lowry Brye is a mom who knows about letting go. Like many moms, she cried when her kids left home, wishes they'd call and write more, and spends sleepless nights worrying about them. But Elaine's tears and concerns are even more poignant than most mothers'—because Elaine is the mom of four military officers, one each in the Air Force, Army, Navy, and Marines.

An Army brat turned ROTC candidate turned military wife, Elaine never expected her kids to have a call to serve, and certainly didn't expect all four to join up. Three of her kids—two sons and a daughter—attended the Naval Academy, and it was there that Elaine got her own calling: she joined the Naval Academy Parents' Listserv, and began a sixteen-year journey of helping moms and dads adjust to their strange, new, lonely lives as military parents.

She also spent a year teaching in Kabul, Afghanistan where she experienced life in a war zone. Her love of her country and desire to support her fellow parents led to her to write "Be Safe, Love Mom: A Military Moms Stories of Courage, Comfort, and Surviving Life on the Homefront," and created BeSafeLoveMom.com to further support and connect those who love their military children.

"Do your duty, love your country, live with honor and suck it up" is her mantra as she encourages military moms to face the challenges and struggles of military life with courage. She co-authored "The Heart of a Military Mom" in hopes that the lessons learned will be empowering and inspirational and provide a reminder that we are not alone in our love, worry and pride for our beloved children.

Made in the USA
San Bernardino, CA
01 July 2018